MW01502984

The Power of Gone

The Power of Gone
Conquering your post-cancer life

BETSY MCFARLAND

Gone Awareness Publishing
P.O. Box 121877, Arlington, TX 76012

ISBN 978-0-9975271-0-0

For my Gone Angels:

To those who are here, I owe you my life.

To those who await me, make yourselves comfortable. It will be a while…

Acknowledgements

A heartfelt thanks goes out to everyone who listened to me whine about getting this book completed – especially to June Shrewsbury and Aimee Leighmayfredrickbob Mouch for helping me with my "process." You deserve your own trophies.

I wouldn't be thanking anyone were it not for the minds and hands of my doctors and their staffs. I quite literally owe you my life. You, too, are my Gone Angels, and please know that you have my undying (no pun intended) gratitude.

Thank you to my editors – formal and informal: Melissa Knox, Susan Clayton, Antonio Godinez, Landa Sloan Orrick, Nan Sprester, Lynne Cox Johnson, Susan Arthur, Robert Ahola, and Tracy Bankston Smith (HRH TJB).

Thank you to Tim Olsen for the massive patience and the beautiful cover.

Thanks, also, to Leo Wesson, photographer extraordinaire, for making me look better than I deserve.

And an especial thanks go out to the family and friends who always knew I had a book in me.

Contents

Foreword: A Snowball's Chance

I am of the opinion that the adage "Life will throw you curve balls" is entirely wrong. I think it is far more accurate to say, "Life will throw rocks at you." Chances are better than good you won't be able to dodge at least one of them and it will likely leave a mark. Those are the moments – at least in my life – that pop psychologists have dubbed defining moments. I take a slightly different view of what defines said defining moment. I believe it is what we do *after* we get hit by that rock that truly defines us.

I got hit by a rock a few years ago, and I chose not to be defined by it, but rather to defy it. This book is my attempt to share that with you and, with luck, inspire you to follow suit should that same rock clobber you.

For years, friends and family have urged me to write a book – any book, whether about my dad, about growing up as a celebrity's child, or about my experiences as an over-50 online dater. This, however, is the first time that a compulsion to write a book has truly gripped me in the gut, heart and mind.

Why? Honestly, this is the first time I have been able to answer the question, "Is this something you're truly passionate about, Betsy?" In the past, I never felt I could do true justice to a biography about Dad (I'll explain this later – hang on!) or that my experiences growing up as my father's daughter were different than any other kid's experience. As for the book about over-50 dating, let's just say I may keep that one in my back pocket for the future. But for this one, the answer was a visceral, "Yes!"

The last 10 years of my life have not been any more remarkable than anyone else's life. I endured an unwelcome divorce from the man whom I thought was the love of my life. I was fortunate to be employed, but the job was a spirit killer. I was diagnosed with cancer. I completed treatments and the cancer is gone, but I will live with the after-effects for the rest of my life – some of which are rather daunting. I was laid off from my job the same week my 85-year-old mother was diagnosed with triple-negative breast cancer just before Thanksgiving of 2014. I have probably stubbed my toes 50 times, broken some heirloom dinnerware, and put my smarter-than-I-am-phone through the spin cycle courtesy of the pocket of my jeans. It's been a whirlwind...

As you read this, you may think, "Holy cow – did that broad break a mirror?" But the truth is, this kind of rock-throwing happens to most of us at one time or another. Yours likely looks different than mine, but it impacted you – or is impacting you now – as much as mine did me. Not more. Not less. Just differently.

I keep a printed quote on the whiteboard in my office. It is from Virginia Satir, an American psychologist, and I reference it frequently:

"Life is not what it's supposed to be. It's what it is. The way you cope with it is what makes the difference."

That may seem like a platitudinous no-brainer, but it is much harder to implement than it might seem at first blush. If you re-examine your own life set-backs I bet you can remember times when sitting in the recliner watching reruns of Hogan's Heroes seemed like the only logical approach you could take to This Rotten Deal.

I did my share of that along the way, but I suppose I'm just not programmed to do that for too long.

FOREWORD

In fact, my career was built on a series of work-for-someone-else, get-laid-off/fired/quit, start-my-own-thing, work-for-someone-else, etc. You get the idea. I have worked for huge, global companies, medium sized national firms, and family-owned enterprises. I have also made money as a communications and public relations consultant, video production assistant, grocery store demo girl (tortilla chips and salsa!) and a talent representative. I have sold toilets and have owned an independent coffee bar. Quite a list, huh?

It is that very tendency – some inner programming to just get busy, if you will, that started a little snowball of an idea on its downhill run.

When I found myself unemployed with an ill mother, was my first inclination to seek out some kind of job that would continue to provide a secure income and group health insurance?

Umm… no.

Rational or not, my first inclination was to take advantage of the free time I now had, trust my cape, and take a flying leap off the top of a scary mountain to start a business based on the idea of nothingness. More to the point at hand, it is based on what I now refer to as *Goneness*.

With a little effort and a whole lot of thinking about it, my little snowball of Goneness has continued to pick up momentum as well as a lot more mass. Some of you may read that as a contradiction – after all, how can nothing become something? To me, it makes perfect sense, and – hopefully – it will to you as well by the time you finish this little book.

This book is a part of that snowball, and whether you feel you are on your own downhill run or if you have already been to hell and back, I hope you will find something in these pages to start creating your own snowball that will surround you like it did me. Wrap yourself up in it, roll around in it, and understand that you are surrounded by the Power of Gone.

For the impatient reader, I have done you a big favor. I am an unapologetic storyteller, so you are about to feel a huge wave of relief wash over you because I will alert you when a story is about to start. You can flip forward until you find *[End of story.]*

You will also find a little postscript at the end of each chapter that I call Take-aways. The Take-aways are the distillation of the message I am trying to convey with each chapter. If you dislike reading, just skip to the end of each chapter, read the Take-aways and be done with it. You will, however, miss out on my uproarious story-telling and heart-warming anecdotes, but to each their own…

TAKE-AWAYS:

1. If the term "take-aways" made sense to you without explanation, you spend way too much time in business meetings. Those things will make you sick.

2. Dodgeball might actually be good practice for dealing with the rest of your life.

1: You're making up words again.

Goneness: a human state of being cancer-free and reveling in it.

Yup, I made it up. Why not? There's a lot of that going on today: biopic, selfie, twerking, etc. With any luck, though, this one may actually serve a higher purpose for you. That is my sincere hope.

Perhaps it will help if I first give you the origin of Goneness. [*Story alert!*]

I turned 50 in 2011, and in August of that year I was diagnosed with stage 3B cancer. Bless her heart, the recovery room nurse accidentally gave me the doctor's report and I had the dubious pleasure of reading about it before the doctor could tell me the outcome.

Curiously, my first thought was not, "Oh God – why me?" Instead, my first thought was, "Well, this is damned inconvenient." Honestly, that was it. Seems a little undramatic – especially for me. Nonetheless, that really was what went through my brain.

Later, when the doc told me that 85% of folks survive this type of cancer with treatment, I knew I would be okay. I was a bit of an academic over-achiever as a kid, so I believed I could pull at least a B on this test. I'm not sure if it was hubris or just ignorance of what was in front of me, but I can say with all honesty that I never once feared for my life.

Truth be told, my greatest fear was not being able to get though it with grace and dignity. Those became my watchwords, and I worked constantly to live up to them. Success was not immediate nor totally consistent, but I knew I had done a creditable job when a co-worker later told me that she admired my "grace and dignity during [my] ordeal." Bingo! Verbatim. Humbling, to say the least.

I must also give credit for my attitude toward the diagnosis to my niece who is a 25+ year Conqueror of childhood leukemia and, at this writing, the mother of two beautiful little heart-stealers. She was three days shy of her third birthday when she was diagnosed. For the next several years, I watched her go through chemotherapy treatments and tests that would make the devil run for cover. I swear that it was as psychologically hard on us adults as it was on her little body.

She lost her hair several times – in fact, we have school pictures of her with little more than fuzz and a headband. But she didn't complain (okay, maybe a little whining on occasion); she… just… did… it. She was my inspiration, and my experience with her is what enabled me to face the diagnosis as a task to be completed rather than a sentence to be suffered.

My feelings about my diagnosis were not shared by everyone, however. I found out later that my own internist had doubts about my survivability. Fortunately for him, he didn't mention those or we would have had a rather serious discussion about his faith in me! My mom, of course, was devastated, but she was as supportive as a terrified mother can be.

I was fortunate to have a number of friends and relatives who worried more about me than I did about myself. (You know who you are, Aimee, Cathy, Keith and Sue!) Several of them conspired behind my back to keep each other informed of concerns or developments, and I admit that I was momentarily vexed when I found out about that – but only for a split second. Intellectually, I knew these folks loved me, but when I heard of the conspiracy I suddenly knew what it was to be truly at the center of someone's heart. I still refer to them as my Gone Angels, and I will explain that later, too.

Fast forward through the chemo and radiation treatments (you are welcome!), and we come to the day when I met with my medical oncologist after the post-treatment CT scan. He informed me that the tests revealed no evidence of cancer in my body.

For anyone who has ever heard those words, you know the feeling I experienced. For those who have been fortunate enough to have never had reason to hear them, let me see if I can find the words to describe the feeling.

- Euphoria
- Joy
- Release
- Elation
- Bliss
- Jubilation
- Ecstasy
- Halleluiah!
- Excitement
- Supercalifragilisticexpialidocious

Nope. All are insufficient.

The only way I can describe it is that I felt as if every cell in my body bloomed into something large, shiny and filled with a bright light. While I am normally happy to use hyperbole, I assure you that this description is actually quite inadequate, but it is the best that I can do with mere words.

So that you don't think I am in a complete state of denial, I did hear the rest of what my doctor told me, and I am fully aware that he never used the word "cured." This is why I happily return once a year for a follow-up scan to prove to him what I already know – that the cancer remains gone.

On my way home from the cancer center – and after I phoned my family and caregivers, I tried to figure out a clever way to tell the rest of my support circle the good news. I decided to post a smart-aleck-y new journal entry on my Caring Bridge site. (Check it out. Everyone should know about and support this terrific resource. www.caringbridge.org).

My post: *"For those of you who know me well, you know that my fashion sense stops at putting together black and white, so I need your help. The various cancer support organizations have these colorful rubber awareness bracelets for each type of cancer. I want a bracelet too, but I don't know what color to get. Since the cancer is now gone, can anyone help me identify the color of gone?"*

I received several notes of congratulations from those who preferred to move past the smart-aleck-y part and get right to the point, but I also received several responses that played along.

A dear friend who is a multi-year cancer Conqueror suggested that the bracelet should be clear – as in my tests were "all clear." A friend who drove me to several treatments after I became too weak to be trusted behind the wheel opined that it should be the colors of fireworks. My sweet aunt said it should be the colors of the rainbow because God heals and God puts the rainbow in the sky for us to enjoy. (I didn't tell her that the rainbow was already spoken for.) Yet another friend who knows me so very well said, "For you, the color of gone is the color of diamonds!"

Each of the suggestions made me smile – and the latter made me laugh out loud, but when I took a moment to think about them I realized something important: diamonds are clear; when you look into a diamond you see fireworks; and when God's sun strikes a diamond it refracts a rainbow. I took this as a sign that the universe intended for me to have a diamond tennis bracelet! I dubbed it my Gone Awareness Bracelet. (I have also subsequently designed and now produce a line of jewelry called The Color of Gone for other Conquerors like me. It is the other half of my snowball.)

I now wear my Gone Awareness diamond tennis bracelet every day, and when I put it on each morning it is my reminder of how I felt when my doctor gave me the news: bright, shiny and filled with light. It is my trophy. It is my reminder of what I can only describe as Goneness. *[End of story.]*

So what exactly is Goneness? Here's the list, but trust me – you'll get a full explanation of each in the subsequent chapters of this book, and perhaps you will find that they have provided you with the building blocks for your own version of Goneness.

- ☆ Goneness is not just a feeling of well-being – though it is that.

- ☆ Goneness is not just a state of health – though it is that, too.

- ☆ Goneness is both of those combined into a rock-solid conviction that the cancer is gone… for good.

- ☆ Goneness is feeling whole, bright, shiny and clean on a cellular level.

- ☆ Goneness is changing the dialogue as well as your inner monologue.

- ☆ Goneness is knowing and celebrating every day for the rest of your life that you have conquered the raging beast of cancer once and for all.

✷ Goneness is celebrating everyone and everything that made your cancer gone.

✷ Goneness is recognizing that you can take the absence of cancer and turn it into something – into anything you wish.

✷ Goneness is unleashing your personal control over your body, your mind and your future.

✷ **Goneness is power.**

TAKE-AWAYS:

1. Do not let fear dictate how you approach a bad situation. Call on history, experience, and faith in yourself to face it and conquer it.

2. If that doesn't work, just make up some new words. At least you will have done something!

2: A rock-solid conviction

I have a pretty good brain. It was better before chemo, but from all reports it is still okay. I have always been good with facts and memory, logic and philosophical musings. Except for a brief period during my teens when Omar Khayyam, Elton John and my ninth-grade health teacher were my philosophers of choice, I have never been a follower of pop-culture gurus or self-help fads. People who know me might say that explains a lot.

However, after my personal d-day (diagnosis day), all of that changed to a certain extent. I was familiar with the "if you can conceive it you can achieve it" school of thought, and I knew on a deep level that I needed to engage my brain's abilities as well as my body's in order to survive the treatments and to fully heal. I also knew that I needed to pray.

Prayer had always been something I did before family meals, at the rare church service that I would attend, and when I passed a roadside accident. I never had anything against it, but it just never had been a big part of my life. Most of us have heard the saying that there are no atheists in a foxhole. I would bet that the same holds true of a chemo infusion room or a radiation suite, whether or not one chooses to admit it.

I admit it.

I am not one to bargain with God – the lady at the antique mall, maybe, but it just seems tacky to haggle with The Big Guy. Rather, I chose to pray for healing, to pray for my doctors and the medical staff to wield their tools wisely, and to comfort my family and friends. Let me state unequivocally that prayer truly does work – at least, it did for me.

When it was all over and the cancer was gone, I knew that it was my turn to make sure that I protected the gift I had been given. I chose to employ my Gone Awareness bracelet to help me with that.

Understand that when I bought the bracelet in January of 2012, it was your standard, run-of-the-mill, everyday, *gorgeous-string-of-sparkly-diamonds-and-*

shiny-gold-that-adorned-my-wrist-to-perfection
typical tennis bracelet.

Yes, the diamonds are clear. Yes, when God's sun hits it, it refracts rainbows. And yes, when I look into it I also see fireworks. It functions perfectly.

What I also see, though, are constant flashes of light every time I move my arm. If I hold very still with my hand in just the right position, it flashes with the beating of my pulse. In very short order, these flashes have come to represent all of the things that allow me to keep breathing and my heart to keep beating.

Its greatest power, though, is its constant presence.

Those of us who have been fortunate enough to win our battle know well that life goes on. We go to dinner and celebrate. Family members throw parties. People hold on to the hug a little longer than usual… for a time. Then the routine of daily life returns for everyone. Please understand that this is not a criticism. In fact, I take it as the highest compliment anyone could give me. It means that I have slogged through the muck of treatment and recovery. It means I have moved past what could easily have become my own giant, personal hog-wallow of self-pity. Instead, some form of normalcy returns and life picks up its usual rhythm – at least that is what people see.

We Conquerors know that isn't *quite* the case, don't we?

Life goes back to normal... but *we* don't. We will always have the memories, and for many of us, we will always deal with the after-effects of the disease and/or the treatments that saved our lives.

Personally, I have some permanent after-effects that I would not wish on my worst enemy. Does their existence anger me? Sometimes, yes, but after a good helping of eye-narrowing, lip-pursing invective, I remember there is no free lunch. I remind myself that these things comprise the price I paid for my life, and the anger recedes. In its place stands a renewed dedication – a rock-solid conviction – to make the most of what I bought for that price.

This conviction has allowed me to give myself permission to be okay with my new normal. Are there things about my old normal that I will miss? You betcha, baby, but I will always believe the trade-off was more than worth it.

TAKE-AWAYS:

1. A certain percentage of my readers don't know what a foxhole is.

2. Don't let unexpected rocks derail your life. Stay the course as best you can and find the value in doing so – regardless of the obscurity of that value.

3: Whole, bright, shiny and clean

If this chapter title makes you think of an Ivory soap ad, I don't blame you. In fact, I kind of like the imagery of a fresh-faced young thing without crows-feet and age spots. Sadly, that's not the kind of wholesome, bright, shiny and clean I'm talking about.

I spoke in Chapter 1 of the feeling I had when I was told the cancer was gone and described it as feeling those things on a cellular level. Far from a scientific or medical state of being, it is rather a state of self-awareness. It is how I *felt.* It is part of the Goneness.

For a while, I wasn't just Betsy. I was also Betsy's tumor, and I was Betsy's radiation burns. I was Betsy's pain, and I was Betsy's complications. I was Betsy's fatigue and Betsy's ennui. Each of those took on a life of its own, and that was a lot of Betsys to keep up with. When the doctor told me the cancer was gone, all of those of Betsys retreated into the part of my brain that holds the dark and unworthy memories. I no longer felt fragmented – I was whole again. I was just one Betsy again.

While those Betsys were retreating, I simultaneously felt as if the light of the sun was trying to burst out of me. It felt like my cells were exploding with that brightness, and I wanted to fly around the room and touch everything with that light.

If you ever watched the movie "Cocoon" and saw Brian Dennehy pull the skin at the corner of his eye to reveal an almost blinding flash of light, try to imagine what that would look and feel like and you might start to understand the sensation I had. It was unlike anything I had ever experienced and is obviously difficult to adequately describe.

We associate brightness with the intensity of light, but that intensity is meaningless unless it has something to reflect off of – our retinas being a prime example. That's where the shiny part comes in. Imagine a chrome bumper in the west Texas August sun. The higher and more direct the sun, the shinier that bumper looks. You've had the experience of looking at something so shiny in the sun that you had to squint or look away. I felt like that kind of shiny.

I was so shiny that all the love and health and luck and healing was reflecting off of me and onto anything and anyone around me.

When I talk about clean, I am talking about the kind that results from a cleansing – mental and physical – of whatever is within you that is causing you distress.

During my treatment and recovery I listened to a CD given to me by a friend. It was a recording of a guided imagery session created by a multi-cancer Conqueror. I listened to it every night as I went to bed and followed his instructions in my mind's eye. So much of what his narrative evoked had to do with running water, the washing away of illness and pain, the bloom of youth and nature, and the immersion of oneself in a feeling of wellness. It may contain other images as well, but I never made it to the end before I fell asleep! To this day, I have no idea what the second half of that CD contains.

Despite my sleep state, I know that my subconscious mind heard and internalized the message because I always knew my treatments were cleansing rather than the more rational feeling of being poisoned. I envisioned the chemo washing around and through my cells to snare and envelope the offending cancer cells and wash them away to make me clean and healthy again. (Or, it is entirely possible that it was all a flashback to watching *"Fantastic Voyage"* as a kid! And, yes, I know that only a small portion of my readers will understand that reference, but it will make them laugh.)

These feelings are aspects of Goneness that are easily lost amidst the return to normalcy with its alarm clocks, staff meetings, carpools and soccer practice. It is only with the mindfulness of intentionally recalling that moment and those emotions that one can fully put the Power of Gone to work. This is why I chose my bracelet as my reminder – my talisman, if you will – of those feelings so I can call upon them at will.

A physician or medical scientist (or even a runner, for that matter) reading this will likely attribute these feelings to a purely physiological response to good news – the release of endorphins into my bloodstream. I won't argue with that. In fact, I quite believe that is the explanation. Regardless of the origin, it is the result of the release that is important. There is not room in the book to cite all of the research that *indicates* endorphins can increase the body's immune response to illnesses. (I got 207,000 hits when I searched "endorphins immune response".)

There is, however, a respectable amount of acceptance in some sectors of both the modern and traditional medical communities that endorphin-producing thoughts can have a positive impact on one's health. I strongly suggest that you do some research yourself on this subject and form your own opinion. I formed mine in 2011 and you should know by now what it is.

If I haven't lost you amid a hail of, "What is this chick smoking?" and "She must be one of those woo-woo types," please understand that I do not smoke anything aside from the occasional rack of ribs and am not a student of the metaphysical arts. I am probably a lot like you – someone who is generally practical and likes to be happy. I am not the kind of person who awakens one day and decides to start preaching about some kind of epiphany, but I am the kind of person who wants to share something that has deeply impacted my life in a positive way with the hope that it might help someone else.

That someone else is you.

TAKE-AWAYS:

1. We have a lot more control over our personal outcomes than we think we do.

2. Make a conscious decision to focus on the positive and take back control of your thinking.

3. Ribs… Yummmmm.

4: Changing the dialogue
...and the monologue

You will never know what kind of cancer I conquered. Unless someone is a medical professional with a practical need to know, I no longer tell anyone where the cancer originated.

If you are a Conqueror, you know the drill: "Oh my. What kind was it/Where was it?" If you are female, the inquisitor inevitably glances down at your chest – because, apparently, our breasts are the only places women develop cancer. Truly, I don't mean to sound flippant, it's just that it happens time and again.

THE POWER OF GONE

I'm the kind of person, though, that gets a little kick out of smiling sweetly while saying, "It was the kind of cancer that's gone," and watching the confusion play across their faces. With the exception of one or two busy-bodies, virtually everyone slowly develops a smile of understanding and responds with something like, "I like that. I get it." At that point I often have the opportunity to step up on my soapbox and gently drop the hint that it is a very personal question (despite society's rather recent penchant for sharing/knowing everything about one another) while explaining the importance of banishing it from my life and celebrating the Goneness.

It can be difficult the first couple of times. Our nature makes us want to answer politely even if, upon reflection, it is truly none of their business. Ask yourself this: which is more important – a conversation about the kind of cancer that attacked you or the fact that you are/were engaged in a battle for your life? I submit to you that it is, was, and always will be the latter. (For those of you still in treatment, get a head start on changing the dialogue and tell them that it is the kind that will be gone as soon as your treatments are complete.)

For most of history (actual and literary), the concept of naming something is thought to give it power and presence. If you're into popular fantasy/fiction, you are aware that the residents of Hogwarts know this ("He

Who Must Not Be Named"), as do the Gondorians who won't speak the name Sauron for fear it will summon him.

While we all know intellectually that these examples are fictitious and based on superstition, how many times in your life have you been talking about someone and they show up? Betcha said something like, "Speak of the devil" and then laughed just a little nervously.

So it was all a big coincidence... probably. I, for one, do not want to take the chance with cancer. It has no name to me because it is gone. It has no presence in my life because it is gone. It has no identity because it is gone.

Some of you reading this may be thinking that all I have done here is to turn "gone" into a euphemism for the type of cancer. You are absolutely right, and I applaud you for realizing that. But it is also a lot more than just a euphemism.

Think of it this way. When you excuse yourself in a restaurant to visit the restroom, I seriously doubt that you say, "Pardon me while I go urinate," or "Excuse me while I go move my bowels." Either or both of those are accurate, but we don't announce it because it is gross, too personal, impolite, in conflict with our upbringing, or all of the above. Society allows us to use euphemisms for these bodily functions so that our companions don't get a great big ol' mental image of what we're depositing in a toilet. So what is the difference between that and redirecting someone's thought process away from your body and toward your victory? After all, your continued presence on this earth and the permanent Goneness of the cancer is much more important than a part of your anatomy or the location of a tumor that may now be residing somewhere in a jar of formalin, yes?

Yes. Yes, it is.

Speaking of manners, make sure that once you tell them the cancer is gone, let them off the hook so they aren't embarrassed for more than a nanosecond. Go on to explain the total gloriousness of your Goneness. If you wish, give them a blow-by-blow of your treatments to satisfy their curiosity, morbid as it may be, but always make sure they walk away knowing as you do that the cancer is gone and will remain so.

Now that we have gently put the general public in their collective place, it is time to work on your own head a little more. You may have noticed that nowhere in this book will the words "my cancer" or "your cancer" appear. You will see "the cancer," instead. Words have meaning, and personal pronouns are just that – personal.

Don't claim it for yourself, and don't give it to me, either! Kick it to the curb like the vile garbage it is.

Cancer is not worthy of the respect that goes along with being one of my or your possessions.

[Gross, but funny, analogy alert! Proceed at your own risk.]

It should be treated the same way one would treat sinus drainage. I bet you've never ever uttered the phrase, "I hocked *my* loogie." For those of you who have never heard of such, in many regions a loogie is a big ol' glob of mucous. If one were to hang out near men's' locker rooms, rodeo arenas, or the front porch of my old high school, one would inevitably hear the unmistakable sound of someone – usually a male – clear said mucous from his throat and spit it out. That would then typically be followed by an appreciative, "Man, did you see that loogie Junior just hocked? Who needs a beer?"

[End of gross analogy. Disturbing analogies on deck.]

If that doesn't quite hit the mark for you, try saying these phrases aloud and see how you feel about them:

* ✶ I am proud that my grandfather killed 15 of his Nazis in WWII.

* ✶ My neighbor's kids were killed in her car accident.

✯ My cut became infected and was oozing
   my pus.

I hope that saying these things made you as uncomfortable as I was writing them. I doubt that anyone's grandfather thinks of a wartime enemy soldier as "his," and it is (thankfully) a social taboo to refer to an accident as "hers" or "his" if it had a tragic outcome. And while our bodies generate white blood cells to fight infection I hope you *never* consider claiming pus as your own. (Besides, it's just a gross word anyway!)

Are you disgusted yet by these last few paragraphs? Good! Then I've made my point that the cancer that attacked you is no more deserving of remaining a part of you than is mucous, pus, an ungodly accident or an evil empire. It doesn't deserve to be spoken of, named or claimed. Ditch the personal pronouns and see how much better you feel.

In the interest of full disclosure, I must tell you that as of this writing, I am still working on this myself. It won't be easy to stop using "my cancer." If you are like me, conquering it became your life's work – quite literally, because it was the most in-your-face, gigantic, attention-hogging thing in your life for the duration of your treatment. You were constantly working to save your life, and that consumed you for a while. Rightly so. You needed to focus on the war, the battles, and the skirmishes to make the cancer gone.

That part is over. Now, you need to be equally committed to maintain the Goneness. The work won't be as hard as the conquering, but changing our thinking is no small feat. If it was, we'd all be buff, gorgeous and bullet-proof.

I spent one semester of my college experience as an advertising major. (Underwhelming, I know.) Two little nuggets of knowledge that were shared with me, however, managed to take up permanent residence: a message must be seen at least three times for someone to internalize it, and it takes the average human 21 repetitions of an action for it to become a habit. (What didn't stick with me is whether this was determined through scientific study or if it was merely the folk wisdom of a Madison Avenue castaway, so forgive me if I don't cite a source.)

Let's do a little math. If we add a few days for not having the time or inclination to participate, and another three or four that fall by the wayside due to hectic schedules, chemo fog or just plain forgetfulness, this adage suggests that we can develop (or, conversely, break) any habit in the course of just one month. Now, let's take that just a little farther. Most habit-forming activities don't require an entire day, but usually fit within a few minutes' time frame. For the sake of argument, let's really stretch it and use 30 minutes per occurrence… 30 minutes times 21…630 minutes divided by 60 minutes… comes out to 10 and a half hours. If we accept the premise (and my math skills), this means that you and I can change our inner monologues and our external dialogues in

LESS THAN ONE-HALF OF ONE DAY!

In the grand scheme of things, that really isn't much of an investment to conquer something negative and create something positive that will impact every waking moment of the rest of your life. I think that qualifies as a bargain.

While we're on the subject of conquering, there's one last change to the dialogue and monologue that I encourage you to make. I suggest that you substitute "conquer" for "survive" and "Conqueror" for "survivor."

Think of other ways we use the word survive. We survive the hurricane. Survivors of the Titanic were rescued from the icy waters. Most Londoners survived the Blitz. In these cases, the attack was something that couldn't truly be fought by the target – too strong, too much of a surprise, better weapons. Basically, those people just hung on or lucked out.

Now think of how we use conquer. There's a reason the term is "conquering hero" not "surviving hero."

Adventurers conquer Everest; those who "survive" it may not have made it halfway before returning to base camp. The conquering hero returns to parades and celebrations; the survivor is quietly hustled in to warm himself by the fire and have his wounds tended.

The line is a fine one, but I contend that survivor connotes a bit of passivity or mere continuity, whereas the term Conqueror brings to mind a warrior who has given his all to overcome the enemy.

I gave my all. I am a Conqueror. You are – or will be, too.

Let go of the cancer survivor and bust out The Conqueror in you. Arm yourself with powerful words, don your mantle of Goneness, and raise your bloody sword of victory like the Conqueror you are. I am standing with you.

TAKE-AWAYS:

1. The words we use are powerful. And sometimes gross.

2. Choose your words wisely and use them like you mean them.

5: Know it! Celebrate it!

The previous chapters have focused primarily upon what has already happened and how I suggest you characterize it while you're having the myriad internal conversations we all have. These concepts are the tenets I am hoping you can internalize and use to your advantage: toss out the garbage of a cancer victim mindset; roll around in the gloriousness of your ability to face another day today; and applaud yourself for winning the battle for your life.

But we aren't finished.

Something rather remarkable happens once you cross the line from cancer patient to cancer Conqueror

– you look at the rest of your life in a different light. Some people see it in a brighter light than others, but I contend that it is virtually impossible not to do so, at least on some level. After all, life has changed – you have changed, and there is no way either it or you can go back to being the same old-same old. That math just doesn't work out. So, it is only fitting that since we have addressed how to deal with yesterday's news and today's situation, it is now time to turn your eyes toward the horizon that is the rest of your glorious life and figure out what it will take to keep you moving toward it.

Self-pity parties, self-doubt, depression, grumpiness – all can be lingering side-effects after cancer. It will likely be up to you – the one with the most to lose – to monitor those feelings and do something about them before they become problematic. They can strike down the most motivated Conqueror if allowed to take up residence – much like a dead-beat brother-in-law. And who wants one of those? It won't always be easy, and many of us will find that the help of a professional is just the ticket. There are some things, however, that we can do for ourselves that can help keep the bum in the basement where he belongs and keep the light inside of us burning brightly. In fact, actively defying those negative effects is one of the most fundamental aspects of the Power of Gone.

Here's a question: At what point in our lives do we stop collecting trophies? I'm not talking about mementoes we have gathered up that hold sentimental value and remind us of happy times, but rather about real trophies of the kind that occupy a three-dimensional space somewhere in our universe.

I am talking about trophies that can be interpreted as nothing else but an award for something done well: loving cups, medals, ribbons, metallic footballs perched atop a column of faux marble and silver-painted plastic. At what point did we stop wanting that physical reward for a job well done? Seriously – think about it for a moment. I'll wait…

There are some of you who immediately glanced over at your mantel or bookcase at a shiny new golf or tennis trophy that you brought home last week. Others looked at the same place and immediately thought, "Are those really cobwebs?" Others, like me, tried to remember which box in which closet holds that 7th grade spelling bee ribbon. And yes, the cobweb comment was mine as well.

We keep those things because they remind us of a moment in time when we were on top, when our best was THE best that day because we trained, sweated, practiced, rehearsed, memorized, bled, and then did it again and again and again until we won the contest or game or match.

We remember the sound of all the people clapping or cheering or whistling. We can picture in our mind's eye the smiling faces of teammates, friends and family beaming with pride because they always knew we could do it. We feel that little rush of something (there are those endorphins again) that makes us feel like we could do that every day for a week. We feel pride. We feel a little smug – come on, admit it. We feel like The Best.

That's why we keep trophies.

Now that you have won the competition of your life – *for* your life, where is your trophy? What is your reminder of that moment in time when you achieved the ultimate triumph – when you became the victor and cancer became the vanquished? What do you have that reminds you of the win in spite of no warning, no chance to rehearse, prepare or practice? What is that thing that you can look at and feel the same elation you felt at the moment you were told you won?

Where is it? Can you look at it every day? Every hour?

What is it? Can you touch it? Can you show it off to the admiring horde? It is something of beauty that makes you smile and feel Good with a capital G?

Or did the fight wear you down to the point where it was enough just to make it through? Good for you, but... not good *enough*, my friend!

Sure, I still treasure the signed tee shirts from my oncology and radiology teams after the completion of my protocols. I work out in them because they make me proud of the fact that I *can* work out again. They aren't trophies, though, because some day they will fade and fray and become cherished dust cloths.

I have read posts on social media from folks who consider their scars to be their trophies. I still have the scar from my port (okay – I asked to save my port, too, but after a few months it just seemed weird). I still have nasty scars from the other surgeries, as well, but for some reason, I really don't feel like I want to put them on display -- and frankly, the public is relieved. Am I ashamed of them? Absolutely not! I just think of them more as by-products of the battle – kind of like sweaty towels, stinky high-tops or divots the size of Manhattan. They are reminders of the battle, but they aren't trophies. They aren't the spoils of war. After all, even those who do not win bear scars. Scars are reminders of the skirmishes, but they are not reminders of my victory... of my Goneness. They don't even come close to making me want to cheer and (try) to jump up in the air to celebrate.

The distinction is fine, granted, but it is a vitally important one. You cannot ever, for one moment of one day of the rest of your life, allow yourself to forget that YOU WON.

YOU WON.

YOU WON.

Say it to yourself right now: "I WON!"

Say it again. And again. And again.

Feels good, doesn't it? There is nothing to be ashamed of. It is better-than-okay to feel that good for the rest of your life.

If you're like me, though, the hard part is remembering to remember — remembering that not only did you fight, but you won. Remembering to celebrate the Goneness. This is where the trophies come in.

Back in the 1970s, there was an ad campaign with a most memorable slogan: "If you don't have an oil well, get one!" Seems pretty simple... if not very practical. But I can, in a very practical way, say to you, "If you don't have a trophy, get one!"

Find a trophy that is substantial – something that you can look at, feel, touch, smell, wrap yourself in or whatever, for the rest of your life. Find a trophy that you can show off, brandish, display, dust or polish. Find a trophy and locate it somewhere that you will see it every day. Find a trophy that celebrates you – not the cancer. Find a trophy that is worthy of your victory – worthy of your Goneness. Find a trophy that will make you mentally pause while that feeling of triumph takes a deep, emotional bow to the personal fan who lives in your own head.

TAKE-AWAYS:

1. Don't ever stop celebrating.

2. Don't ever stop celebrating.

3. Don't ever stop celebrating.

6: Everyone and Everything

"You simply will not be the same person two months from now after consciously giving thanks each day for the abundance that exists in your life. And you will have set in motion an ancient spiritual law: the more you have and are grateful for, the more will be given you."
— *Sarah Ban Breathnach*

I mentioned in Chapter 1 that my trophy bracelet is made of diamonds that remind me constantly of the people who made the cancer gone.

Being made of diamonds, the bracelet has an infinite supply of sparkles. There is a flash for every prayer that anyone said for me, every meal that was prepared and delivered to my door, every ride to treatment, every class that my doctors took to learn what they did, every phone call, every note on my Caring Bridge page, every conversation with my boss and my co-workers assuring me that it would all be waiting for me when I returned, every hug, every kiss, every well-wish. They represent all the things that made the cancer gone.

I have worn that bracelet almost every day since then. I lock it up for trips to third-world countries and I don't wear it when I'm stuffing a turkey. Other than that, it is a rare occasion when it is not on my wrist.

I say a little prayer of thanks when I put it on in the morning. I also say another at night when I take it off. When I spy it from the corner of my eye while unloading the dishwasher it reminds me that the cancer is gone. When I have that hand at two-o'clock on my steering wheel and the sun is glinting off of it, I smile because my blessings are dancing in the sunlight and I know with every fiber of my being that the cancer is gone.

During treatment, there were times when I couldn't do for myself very well, and people who love me were there to pick up the slack. I was always grateful and more than a little relieved when I didn't have to schlepp the laundry up and down the stairs, figure out where to find the energy to push in the clutch pedal 40 or so times to get to the clinic, wash my car, drag myself through the produce aisle or even make a decision to call the doctor about a fever. Whenever I truly needed them, someone was inevitably there.

Just as science and the administration of that science conspired to kill the cancer, the love and concern swirling around me conspired to save my life. The people responsible for both conspiracies are now referred to as my Gone Angels, as I truly believe that only an army of angels could care that much, give that selflessly, and turn the tide to my advantage – all with no guarantee of success or reward.

When I see a person who did something to make the cancer gone, I always try to take the opportunity to let them know how they are forever a part of what life I have left, and I attempt to show them that I will revel in and not squander their gift.

There is no way I can adequately repay any of them for their efforts other than to thank them and LIVE – live well, live happy, live with intentional gusto.

Doing this, though, can be challenging on any day: bills arrive, your parade gets rained on, the dog permanently redesigns your designer shoes, you just don't want to finish writing that chapter, or a million other irritants crop up that can darken the brightest life. But isn't that kind of the point?

If not for the fact that you are still here, you wouldn't even have those designer shoes. You wouldn't have plans for the parade. You wouldn't have even had the chance to incur those pesky bills. How gloriously alive you are!! And how gloriously fortunate you are that there are people in this world – and more specifically, in your life, who find that expending a little energy in your direction is worth it to save your blessed hide.

Wow. And yippee, by God!

For me, it is this feeling of gratitude for my Gone Angels that is captured in my trophy and how it constantly reminds me of everyone and everything that had role in my Goneness. Talk about abundance!

I have found, as the lady quoted at the beginning of the chapter says, it is true that I am no longer the same person I was before I started being grateful for that abundance. She is one smart cookie.

TAKE-AWAYS:

1. Count your blessings. (Not original, but ancient… for a reason.)

2. Count them again.

3. Thank them for having that role in your life.

7: Nothing into something

My mom is a remarkable human being. She is the only person I know who can go to someone else's garage sale and make money. Seriously. She bought a pair of embellished socks for her granddaughter, and as she was walking away she decided they were cute but too small. Just as this occurred to her, another lady chased her down and asked if she had seen any others like them on display. Mother said no and promptly offered them to the lady for twice what she paid. Cha-ching!!

She is also the only person I know who could look at an empty carpet spool and see it as a totem pole for my third-grade class's project on Native American culture. Mom was every teacher's dream Room Mother.

She is, and always has been, someone who can take nothing – or virtually nothing – and turn it into something of good use or value. Is it because she is a child of the Great Depression raised on a farm in dust-bowl Oklahoma? Is it because she has this innate gift for seeing great potential in the otherwise mundane or valueless? Probably some of both, but it boils down to her ability to see a need, assess what she has – or doesn't have, for that matter, and get busy turning that nothing into something. It's all about identifying an opportunity and making the most of it.

It is the same with harnessing your Goneness.

Since we have determined that you can unleash your Goneness with intestinal fortitude and ferocity, we might want to consider what it is that you could be unleashing it upon. This is that part that will require you to do a little dreaming and a lot of self-talk. The dreaming part is easy, the self-talk might involve a bit more effort – but it will be completely worth it.

Ask yourself some version of the following questions: What is the nothing? What is missing? What is the something I will create from that nothingness? Translated: What opportunity has this experience given me that my Goneness will empower? What is it I have always wanted to do?

THE POWER OF GONE

Is there some idea you thought of ten years ago but never acted on because you had other really important things to do… like climb a corporate ladder or even just binge watch a cable TV series? Hmmm? It could be a little thing; it could be a great big hairy thing that scares the bejeezus out of you just to think about; it could be anything in between.

Whatever it is, DO NOT be afraid to identify it, bounce it around in that noggin of yours, and ask yourself, "Why not? Why not me?" Write down those questions.

After you have asked those questions, ANSWER THEM! This is the step that I never took before.

Start with, "Why not?" Is it illegal? Is it immoral? Will it make you gain 50 pounds overnight? Somehow, I doubt it.

Is there something about it so complex you can't break it down to its elements and tackle those one at a time? Don't assume that until you have given it your best shot. Is it so far out of your intellectual capacity that you can't go online/go back to school/read a book about it to learn what you need to know? Probably not, so go get a library card and start reading.

Is someone standing in front of you, armed to the teeth and preventing you from taking action? If so, give them a swift kick in the dangly bits and move on.

Is it something so expensive that you'll have to live out of your grandfather's 1983 Dodge station wagon? That's what the Small Business Administration or a financial counselor is for. Find one and get busy.

Next question: "Why not me?" Quite honestly, there is no acceptable answer for this one. Not one. If not you, then why are you still here, huh? You overcame tremendous odds that, sadly, so many do not. On their behalf, I implore you not to squander that gift. Life has written you– yes, YOU – a big, fat, blank check, and you would be a fool (a harsh term, I know) not to cash it.

Then ask yourself one last question: "Why not now?" Let's do something together: have a seat and take off your shoes/boots/mukluks/flip-flops, dust off the lint or sand, and read aloud the expiration date printed on the sole of your foot. Whaaaaat? There is no expiration date printed there? Glory be, say it ain't so!

But wouldn't it be nice if we knew that date so we could stop procrastinating and get those things done on our list of Things To Do Before We Expire? (I would use a more popular phrase having to do with a bucket, but I fear it may infringe on someone's copyright or I may have a reader from the Planet Glerf who has never heard of such.) Sure, that knowledge would be nice, but my point here is that we don't have the first clue when that day or that hour or that minute will come.

Those of us who are Conquerors may understand that better than anyone. You came face to face with the last page of your life calendar, but you firmly refused to tear it off. You got another day.

I refer to these days as my Bonus Days. I admit that it took me well over 900 of my Bonus Days to make the decision that eventually led to the series of actions that are culminating in this book. I'm still kicking myself for waiting that long, quite frankly. I don't want that for you. I want you to embrace this fresh, clean calendar and do something TODAY that is worthy of a Conqueror.

So, what are you gonna do with it? How will you fill the gift box of that day and every day to follow it? Will you be grateful just to have the opportunity to go back to the comfort of your old routine, or will there be some nagging at the back of your brain suggesting that maybe, just perhaps, there's something different you're supposed to do? I challenge you to invest a little bit of time – an hour will probably do the trick – to spend some quiet time reflecting on these questions. There is no right answer, but I have the feeling you already know it… if you're honest with yourself. This is your chance – right this very moment – to take your first baby step.

Here is another little exercise that we can do
together. The lines below are for you to take a couple
of minutes and jot down two things that complete the
sentence, "Boy, if I only had the time, energy,
motivation and cash to…"

1. _____

_____

2. _____

_____

(If you are reading the electronic version of the
book, please grab a cocktail napkin for this. Urban
legend has it that the best ideas are scribbled on
cocktail napkins. Why take the chance with a mere
notepad?)

If I were a gambler, I would bet that one of your
ideas is quite audacious and the other is the one that
you subconsciously said, "I'll add this because it isn't
as grandiose, and I might actually be able to do it."
Think about it. I betcha did that. Let's address that one
first.

Read it two or three times. Now cross it off. We're
done with that one. It isn't worthy of a Conqueror, and
you can always do it for an encore.

Now for the big Mamma-Jamma. The Big Scary. The Thing You Really Want To Do But Are Afraid To Admit To Anyone.

The first thing I want you to do is to admit it to someone. Say the words out loud to a trusted human. If they laugh, give 'em the old Bronx Cheer and go find a more trusted human – someone who knows your heart and is so very happy that you are still around to dream big. Next, explain to them

- this is no longer a dream;
- it is a goal;
- it will have a plan;
- the plan will have a timeline;
- the plan will be executed according to the timeline;
- you will succeed.

They didn't laugh, did they? People react in completely different ways to the statement, "I think I would like to…" versus, "I have created a plan to…" Dreamers wait for fate to intervene; Conquerors create battle plans. Simple as that – and I speak from experience.

Throughout my adult life, I have had many, many Great Ideas that I just knew the marketplace would clasp to its collective breast, praise me for my brilliance, and finance my retirement villa in Belize. Today, I can remember only three of them. Why did I forget the others? I forgot them because I failed to do a couple of really important things like give them names or make plans. Of those I remember, I can tell you all three had names and two had plans. I actually launched the two that had plans. (Someday, I may get around to formulating a plan for Bucket O' Panties and do that for my encore. I'll let you know.)

Do you remember the reference in Chapter 4 to speaking of the devil and why I now refuse to say the name of the killer whose butt I kicked into oblivion? Let's review.

The same – but inverse – theory applies here. Giving something a name gives it an identity. A name makes it real. Just as you will never forget the names of your children, naming your goal will ensure that it doesn't disappear into the moldering mental card catalog that is your memory. A name will also serve as a sort of shortcut to the part of your brain that processes emotions and (here we go again) calls for the release of endorphins. Memories that are tied to emotions tend to stick with us longer than, say, the Pythagorean Theorem, despite the fact that it has a name... a completely unpronounceable name.

So give your goal a name, and make it a good one. One of the ideas that I launched was a coffee bar and art gallery that I called The Art of Espresso. To me, the name implied a certain atmosphere that allowed me to envision what the place might look like inside, and that made the planning soooo much easier.

Bear in mind that not all goals will involve a commercial product or enterprise. When we were 16, a dear friend of mine from high school (also a cancer Conqueror) said she wanted to become an astronaut. If she were to use that as her goal today, I would recommend calling it something like Operation Moonwalk because the words, "I am launching Operation Moonwalk" just sounds more powerful, doable and *real* than, "I want to be an astronaut."

If your goal is something like losing 40 pounds, think about all the wonderful things that follow on the heels of achieving this goal: a new wardrobe, easier breathing, less painful knees, a more enjoyable sex life, etc. Don't just say, "I want to lose 40 pounds." Instead, call it "The Stud Finder Plan" or "Mission: Bustier." Besides, one just cannot whine convincingly when saying "stud finder."

Now that you have named your goal, it's time to plan. This is especially crucial for those of you who initially felt that the project was too complex or you don't have the proper body of knowledge. Allow me to say that the sun has set on the Day of the Encyclopedia, and learning how to do something now is the digital equivalent of child's play. Going back to Operation Moonwalk, I did an Internet search for "How to apply to the space program." Within 0.52 seconds, my screen showed the first of 72 million results, and the first eight or so had the letters NASA in the URL. Houston, we have ignition.

Pun fully intended, none of this is rocket-science, Buzz. It may be time-consuming, but aren't most things that are worth pursuing? In this fairly new century we have so much information (some of it is actually accurate!) at our fingertips that one can gain access to the fundamentals of just about anything before you can say, "Liftoff!"

When I decided to launch my coffee shop I had never worked in food service, couldn't order a latte without getting a bad look from some kid with too much hardware in his eyebrows, and my mother almost wet herself laughing when I said I was opening an art gallery. But I researched coffee, coffee suppliers, coffee bar equipment and systems for displaying art. I read some books, found some art experts, enlisted the help of my very talented husband/craftsman, and set a date for opening. Once I started creating this shop, I found I couldn't stop. In fact, it took on a life of its own and I truly felt that it only needed me around because someone had to answer the phone.

My latest venture was no less foreign. The idea of me designing jewelry was almost as funny as opening an art gallery (for many of the same reasons). My jewelry expertise consisted of the fact that I wore jewelry and the diamond is my birthstone. My only retail experience occurred during a six-week period in 1977 when I was hired as Christmas help at a household goods store.

In summary, I started this business from a state of nothingness. I knew nothing about this thing I wanted to do, I had no talent to render what my creativity produced, and I didn't have enough of my own money to make it happen. Nevertheless, I gave it a name, did my research, created a plan, and I am now executing that plan. I have never been so excited-gratified-terrified in my life. But, boy! Do I ever feel alive, and I know that this is what Goneness feels like. I know that I can take nothing and, with a little planning, turn it into something. I really want you to know it, too.

TAKE-AWAYS:

1. You have defied one of the most prolific killers on earth. Now it is time to make the rest of your life into what you always wanted it to be.

2. You can do anything you wish, but you must have the guts to give it a name and the conviction to build a plan for it.

3. The dictionary in my word-processing software does not recognize bejeezus as a word.

8: "Unleash the hounds!"

Congratulations! Like Zeus giving birth to Athena through his forehead (gaaaaack!!), you have now given mental birth to the thing that will define your Goneness (assuming you chose to play along with me in Chapter 7). You have named it, and you have a plan for its life. Great work. Now the hard part begins.

Sorry.

Now that you have decided to make this quantum leap into the new and exciting life that you have been granted, your old life shows up and stows away to come along for the ride. Likely, you have re-acclimated to the old life already, so it could be a challenge to keep yourself motivated to keep moving forward instead of falling back into the well-worn recliner of your pre-cancer life.

You cannot let that happen. (It happened to me for a time, and I finally sought the help of an executive coach.) Remember – to the victor go the spoils, and you deserve a little spoiling. I want you to make the most of this new life and I want you to achieve that goal!

Use your Goneness to help with this. Use its power to unleash your personal control over your body, your mind and your future. It won't happen magically, of course. You have to participate.

Try this: visualize a bunch of horses milling about in front of a manor house, complete with English gentry tricked out in their red hunting jackets and jodhpurs waiting to go crashing through glen and thicket after a bunch of baying dogs pulling at their leads. Can you see the mist at the tree line? Can you hear the French horns (or bugles, or whatever they are) blowing "puh-PAHHHH! puh-PAHHHH" and some guy off-camera shouting, "Unleash the hounds!" Then they will all– veddy, veddy politely, of course, fall in behind the one guy who knows where they have laid down the trail of chemical fox scent (they have outlawed the real thing) and go galloping off to fulfill their cultural imperative. And there you are – galloping right alongside some earl or other with the distant sound of the dog pack, the steed at stride beneath you, and the crisp, autumn wind threatening to pop that funny little helmet-hat-thingy right off your head into the brook you just jumped. I would like for you to keep this image top of mind while you read the rest of this chapter. It is relevant, I promise.

"[sigh] Nice imagery, Betsy, but just how do you propose I go about this? Why do you think I could do this now if I wasn't able/willing to do it before?"

Forgive me, but allow me to turn that right around on you, sister/mister. How do YOU propose to do this? Why do you think you CAN'T do it? Huh? Why not?? You just KO'd the Grim Reaper, my friend. Do you not yet understand what a remarkable undertaking that was? Do you not just giggle uncontrollably that you beat the odds? Do you not walk around grinning like the village idiot because you were stronger, tougher and badder than something that kills people every single day? You oughtta be, baby. You have earned the right to do all of those things… and more.

You have earned the right to unleash the strength and beauty of that body that came through the maelstrom of chemicals and radiation. You have earned the right to let loose the power of that herculean will that resides between your ears. You have earned the right to pursue a future painted in any way that brings you the most joy, fulfillment, gratitude and glee.

Spend some time identifying the things that you want out of life that might have been back-burnered or that you didn't pursue due to perceived time constraints, inconvenience, or a fear of inadequacy or ultimate failure. Pinpoint them. Target them. Then, unleash those Hounds of Goneness on their butts! Trust me – if you trumped Stage Anything Cancer, you can learn to tap-dance, start your dream business, plant a community garden, or go live in the Amazonian rainforest to study poison-dart frogs. Those only require a new pair of noisy shoes, a laptop and an Internet connection, a seed catalog and a hoe, or a couple of vaccinations from your local health department… and maybe some heavy-duty mosquito netting. Small potatoes when compared to what you have come through since none of those activities require the wielding of an actual will to live, experimental drugs, surgeries, photon beams or port-a-caths.

The overriding purpose of this chapter is not to tell you how to go about any of this but rather to tell you how I did it – and perhaps you can find a tool or two here that you'd like to borrow. Besides, there are enough authors and motivational speakers to sink a small continent who know a lot more than I do about self-motivation, and they would all dearly love to help you. What I do know is that I have been able to make my leap by calling on my own history, my knowledge of myself, and the things I have learned from people I know, love and respect – with a big, heaping-helping from one person in particular.

For those of you who haven't already skipped to the "About the Author" section at the end of this book, allow me to introduce you to someone that has always had an enormous impact on my life—despite the fact that he has been gone for more than two decades, but who is also the one whose teachings and legacy continue to inspire, encourage and challenge me in so many, many ways, including my will to survive cancer. Many of you know him as Spanky of Little Rascals and Our Gang Comedies fame – that precious and precocious little cherub that helped bring America through the drudgery and despair of The Great Depression.

I called him Daddy.

The whole story of his life would fill another volume or two, but I can briefly tell you that the story of my life would not be complete without giving him a great deal of the credit for my ability to continue writing it.

My dad was the quintessential self- reinventor. In fact, I like to think that he invented personal reinvention. (Okay, I know he didn't, but his name should be somewhere on the patent.)

[Story alert!]

He started his career in Dallas, Texas, modeling baby clothes and serving as a subject for an aunt's commercial art endeavors. Another of his aunts submitted his photos and bio to the Hal Roach Studio in Hollywood as they were constantly searching for new talent to add to "the gang." Ultimately, he was hired and made his film debut at the ripe old age of three.

Between 1931 and 1942, he made 95 of the classic short-subject films as well as a handful of full-length feature movies. He was, as they used to say, a hot commodity... but for a very short time. He turned 14 in 1942, and although he still looked youthful, his voice was changing and his beard was starting to come in. In other words, he outgrew himself.

Much like today, screen writers and audiences alike didn't have much use for a chubby leading man who looked 10 but sounded like he was well into his teens. His dad tried "shopping" him to studios for secondary roles, but he was too well known by that time. Eventually, the family packed up and moved back to Dallas where they resumed what most would call a "normal" life.

His first post-Hollywood reinvention had him joining the Army Air Corps and serving in San Antonio, Texas, at the end of World War II. During his hitch, his father developed severe emphysema and was unable to provide for my grandmother and the two youngest children. Dad asked for and was granted a hardship discharge to go back and, once more, support the family.

He worked where he could over the next several years including with a major defense contractor in the Dallas area. After several years, he decided to try Hollywood again as a 20-something young man. He did myriad other jobs as did other aspiring actors, but in his own words, he "couldn't get arrested"—his euphemism for not being able to find work as an actor. Nevertheless, he stuck with California for several years, and it was during this time that he met and married my mother.

He knew that he had to do something else to support her and a new son, so he put the acting aside and worked selling cars, and at one point even worked in an ice cream factory.

An opportunity arose in Wichita, Kansas, to make personal appearances and sell autographs, so they packed up and moved to the heartland where he returned to being Spanky. Shortly after that, he landed a job as the host of an afternoon children's program called "Spanky's Clubhouse" in Tulsa, Oklahoma. It was a great experience for him, that is, until the station replaced his show with "The Three Stooges." You wouldn't have heard a lot of nyuk nyuk-ing at his house at that point.

By that time, he had been out of the Hollywood scene for more than 15 years, and he was ready to try something else. Like most other folks who successfully re-invent themselves, he first assessed his skills and abilities, albeit he had to focus on those that didn't involve acting. He felt that corporate sales might be a good match, and he pursued and secured a job with a wine company as a salesman.

With the exception of a few years during which he operated a barbecue restaurant and then a nightclub, corporate sales became his chosen career. He was very good at it because he worked his tail off, and he supported us very comfortably well into the 1980s. There were times when he didn't like his boss, or the company had shifted his territory, or his quotas had been increased by ridiculous amounts, but he kept at it.

He worked harder at that than anyone else I have ever known in my life. He had his office in our house, and I can remember as I left for school he usually would be sitting in his bathrobe at his typewriter pecking away with two fingers, a cup of coffee at his elbow, and his hair standing on-end. I would come home in the afternoon and, very often, he would be in the same place, hair still in disarray, with the coffee, cold, still at his elbow. Then he would be gone for a week at a time to work his territory and fulfill the obligation to his customers and his employer. I daresay that most kids believe their parents work hard, but I had a front-row seat and witnessed first-hand just what that looked like.

Around 1985, he and I developed a program called "A Little Bit of Nostalgia" for the lecture circuit, and he became a very popular guest on college campuses sharing his story and showing film clips. About that same time, he became quite in-demand on the celebrity/charity golf tournament circuit due to his love of the game, his commitment to the idea that celebrities should give back, and the fact that people just really wanted to meet Spanky. By that time, he had been working for more than 50 years and he wasn't even 60 yet. *[End of story.]*

So to recap, this guy's career looked something like this:

- Actor
- Airman
- Factory worker
- Car salesman
- Former actor
- TV show host

- Wine salesman
- Restauranteur
- Barman
- Salesman
- Former actor/guest lecturer
- Pretty darned good golfer

That list is why I say he virtually invented re-invention. Making the choice to do that is, as far as I have been able to observe, something that one can do successfully, and his ability to model that for me has been invaluable during my lifetime.

Understand that this legacy has so many facets, but those that carried me through were those that taught me you never give up just because life throws rocks:

> ☆ It doesn't matter what you did yesterday. Today and tomorrow are the days to which you have a responsibility;

> ☆ Figure out what you are good at and use it to make a difference;

> ☆ Get off your butt and get busy.

His real-life example is what gave me the post-cancer confidence to embark on my own foxhunt, if you will. He blazed the trail that allowed me to reinvent myself in a way that honors the efforts of my Gone Angels and my own victory. I also hope I honor him by doing it the right way, for the right reasons, and by doing it well.

Now that you have read about one source of my inspiration, it is your turn to look inward and find those examples, those legacies, those character traits that you can call upon. This time in your life – this right-now, is your golden opportunity to mount the horse of Goneness, take the metaphorical reins of your life, race to the front of that pack and chase down the fox that is your dream life.

Tally ho!!

TAKE-AWAYS:

1. Conquering cancer changes us, but we have the power to make it a change for the better.

2. The sum of our life experiences and the legacies that have been left to us are the tools we always carry with us for building that better, happier and more fulfilling life.

3. Betsy can torture a metaphor until it crawls whimpering back to its den.

9: Goneness is Power

In *Walden,* Henry David Thoreau said, *"The mass of men lead lives of quiet desperation... But it is a characteristic of wisdom not to do desperate things."* There were a couple of other sentences in the middle about muskrats and such, but they aren't very germane to our topic... for obvious reasons. Thoreau was referring to single-minded economic pursuits, but the same could be interpreted to apply to many survivors (term used intentionally) of this nasty disease.

Some folks spend the gift of their lives worrying about its return or fretting about their scars or limps or new dietary restrictions. They are desperate to survive, but they forget to actually live with intent. Embracing

Goneness can help abolish the desperation brought on by fear and, dare I say, self-pity, and it allows you to pursue a life with positive intent.

In the previous chapters, I have attempted to define for you what Goneness is, why it is not just important but completely necessary to me, and how you, too, can harness it to enrich this most incredible new chapter/act/episode of your life. I tried to give you some meaningful examples (and bombarded you with metaphors!) that could help you apply each aspect to your own situation.

Now that we have looked at them each through a microscope, let's step back and look at how they build upon each other and fit together to create the big picture of a life lived wisely.

What have we accomplished so far?

We have recognized and embraced that we are well again. We feel renewed and refreshed because we now have the ability to summon that image of being bright, shiny and clean at any time we choose to do so.

This is where it starts, because the other steps rely heavily on our own willingness to accept the premise of our return to good health. Practice this regularly – even after you have embraced Goneness because it is so easy to slip back into the habit of focusing on this ache or that pain or that pesky gnat of fear. Besides, it feels soooo good to feel good, doesn't it?

You have added a new word to your daily vocabulary: Conqueror. Now, there's a word with power! Are you standing on a mountain top lifting your bloodied sword in victory? Are you surveying the new kingdom that is the rest of your life? Get that mental image burned into your brain. You have earned the title of Conqueror and I challenge you to use it unashamedly in place of the word survivor. Let me know if anyone objects.

You have also made the conscious decision to remove a word from your vocabulary and simultaneously put cancer in its place by depriving it of a name. It is vital to remember that giving cancer the gift of a name is, in a very real way, giving it more power than it has already claimed. It tried to take your life – remember? So strip it of its identity and let it go slithering back into the black hole of oblivion.

Once you have freed yourself from that bit of mental nastiness, you have the freedom to shift your focus from merely "surviving with a history of cancer" to celebrating your Goneness with wanton revelry. (Okay, maybe not wanton, but certainly exuberant.) Because it is never as much fun to celebrate alone, you now have a very tangible list of those who deserve to celebrate with you. You have counted them as your blessings (and then recounted them, yes?), and it's time to strap on the party hat of gratitude and remind them at every opportunity how they, too, are responsible for your Goneness.

Speaking aloud of your gratitude is immensely healing, and just imagine what it is doing for them to know that you acknowledge and cherish their love, kindness and skill. If you have not been able to free yourself from the belief that you aren't healthy and are still shackled by Fill-in-the-blank-Cancer-of-the-Whatsit, then your words of gratitude will not be the gift that you hope them to be. Think of it this way: would you want to be thanked for helping deliver someone to a life filled with fear and black clouds? So do them all a favor and celebrate these days in full appreciation and self-fulfillment. It will be the best thank-you gift you could give them.

In this same vein, you also can now call upon examples from your own life of the people and circumstances that help you model new ways to dodge the rocks being hurled at you. Personal legacies, stories of victory, and anecdotes of guts-and-glory in the headlights of oncoming challenges are all weapons in your arsenal now. Wield them constantly to deflect the negativity, disappointment and fear that you may encounter on your way to Goneness.

Finally, you have committed to acquiring a trophy for all this trouble you have gone through. Its purpose is to constantly remind you of your victory. It is the laurels for the Conqueror. It will be beautiful and physical and will occupy a place that you will see it every day – preferably all day. This trophy will be worthy of your battle; it will be worthy of your life. It will be a worthy and powerful symbol of your Goneness.

I bet Mr. Thoreau would agree that this is the wise thing to do.

TAKE-AWAYS:

1. Don't hang out with muskrats. Apparently, they breed despair.

2. Allow yourself to be well again. It is the best thing ever.

3. Claim the Power of Gone for yourself. You have earned it. Tap into it.

10: Tied up in a bow

…or, The Ultimate Take-Aways

The title of this chapter might lead you to believe that I am going to bring all messages of the preceding chapters together into one nice, tidy, beribboned little package of wisdom that you can put on a shelf and take down occasionally to behold. Sorry – joke is on you. First, there is very little in this life that can be wrapped up like that. Second, I'm not good with bows.

Life is untidy and often not very nice. There are so many things happening around us every minute of every day there isn't enough ribbon in the world to wrap up all the wisdom we need just to get from sun-up to sun-down. The best I can hope for is that something between these pages has made you think, given you encouragement, or made you laugh.

Second, the bow I am referring to is not on something from me to you. It is, rather, a bow that I want you to put on your Goneness… and then give it away.

The day you start living life using the Power of Gone is the day that others start perceiving in you a fundamental change. They will see in your eyes a renewed light. They will sense a strength that they perhaps have not seen since your d-day. They will know that you are back from the brink and fully intend to stick around.

For those that love you (on whatever level), that is a priceless gift, and one that, quite frankly, you owe them. Let them see the light in you that is guiding you down the path to this most precious part of your life – whatever you choose it to be. Let them see the fear disappearing until it isn't even a memory – just a bad dream from which you have awoken whole, bright, shiny and clean.

My friends and family perceive this in me, and no one even asks anymore if I'm feeling good or how my annual tests came out. They already know the answers to these questions because they see it in my eyes, they hear it in my words, and they sense it in my demeanor.

Far from hurting my feelings, I delight in the absence of their worry. (Except for my mom. She's a mom, so she's hardwired to worry!)

When my mom was diagnosed, she told her oncologist that she wanted to get started right away with her treatments because, as she said, "I just want it to be GONE." She then looked over at me, smiled bravely, and said, "Right, Betsy?" I knew then that my Goneness is a real thing that others can perceive and that it is inspiring to those who need it. The fact that it was my own mother still brings tears to my eyes.

As I said before, words are powerful and "gone" has become one of the most powerful in my arsenal.

Be that model for others who are going through their own battles for their lives. Show them what it looks like to no longer fear their own mortality. Show them that they, too, can live with Gone just as easily – and a lot more happily – than they can live with doubt and despair. Be the person they want to be when their doc tells them they are cancer-free. It really is a wonderful gift.

Don't limit yourself, though, to only those who have gone to battle against cancer. As we all know too well, the Conqueror doesn't fight alone.

Don't be surprised if the energy of Goneness emanating from you inspires others to apply it to their own circumstances. I ask that you be open to allow others to interpret Goneness in ways that are meaningful to their life circumstances. However you or others choose to define Goneness, it can be a powerful, positive force in your life and the lives of those around you.

My mother's cousin embraced Goneness as a way to honor her late mother who had conquered late-life cancer. She lived many years afterward, and this cousin uses Goneness (and the trophy she bought) to remind herself of her mother's strength, tenacity, Goneness and longevity – she lived to be 101.

You should also know that some battles worthy of Goneness have nothing at all to do with cancer. The day I received the prototypes of my jewelry designs, I stopped in at a local restaurant for some lunch (and perhaps a margarita). I didn't want to leave the jewelry in the car – and I did want to inspect/admire it – so I took the case inside and spread the collection out on the table between the fajitas and the guacamole. The manager there asked about it so I told him the story behind The Color of Gone and my plans for the jewelry and for this book. He immediately grasped the concept of Goneness and expressed an interest once I had things up and running. I asked if he or someone close to him was a cancer Conqueror. He replied that he was not, but rather that his doctor had recently declared him to be HIV-negative. He opened my eyes at that moment to the universality of Goneness and how it truly can be applied outside of the cancer Conqueror circle.

As exemplified by these two examples, Goneness can be applied to so many things that have nothing to do with cancer, whether it is another life-threatening disease, a life-changing event, or just a really, really rotten day. Regardless of the issue, the concept remains the same.

Share your Goneness with those who may still be struggling with the fear of a recurrence or maybe with someone who has hit a rough emotional patch during their treatment.

Be that person whom others look to as an example of glorious Goneness. Be the Conqueror that others want to emulate. You will be amazed at the changes you will see in yourself and in those around you when you harness the Power of Gone.

To learn more about Betsy McFarland's line of
fine jewelry for Cancer Conquerors, visit her website at

www.TheColorOfGone.com

About the Author

Betsy McFarland is a jewelry designer, producer and public speaker. She lives in Fort Worth, Texas, loves to relax in the Texas Hill Country, scuba dive off the coast of Belize, and is learning to appreciate single malt whisky.

Betsy's parents discovered early on that she might never shut up, so they enrolled her in a performing arts kindergarten and she's been looking for a stage and microphone ever since. Her inner ham is a genetic imperative as she is fortunate to be the child of the late Spanky McFarland, ringleader of the Little Rascals and Our Gang comedies.

Her line of fine jewelry, The Color of Gone®, is a unique concept in the world of awareness jewelry for cancer Conquerors. Its purpose is to be the trophy for the Conqueror and to celebrate the wearer's victory over cancer – to be the symbol of Goneness. It can be found at www.TheColorOfGone.com.

She holds a fine arts degree from Texas Christian University and earned her MBA at the University of Dallas.